This Book
belongs to

_____

Urgent Plea!

Thank you for purchasing our book. Please be kind
and write a REVIEW of this book on Amazon.
We need your feedback to make the
future books better. Thank you so much!

Pick up all of the exciting books in the Adventures of Alex and Andi series including:

1. I'm A Big Sister Now! The Adventure Begins.

    ★   The book that started it all. Join Alex and Andi on their first adventure together.

2. Who Are Two Special People?

    ★   A fun guessing game about Grandma and Grandpa with clues to lead you along the way.

3. From Daddy to Baby Girl

    ★   A special message from any Father to his precious little Girl.

4. Swing

    ★   Have a favorite pastime? So do Alex and Andi. Come along for a fun ride in this exciting tale that will swing your imagination to a joyful place.

★★★Just to say thanks for purchasing our books, go to the page below to learn how to get FREE copies of new releases in the Alex and Andi Series★★★

AlexAndiAdventures.com/Gift

To Chulees, our dooga, our friend, our family.
Thank you for all of the wonderful years and memories.
We will miss you!
09/13/13

I always wondered if it was
true since the time
when I was just about seven,
"Can it be true that after life
all dogs they go to heaven?"

Many years had passed me by
and I was a child no more,
I became a dad to Brittney;
what fun we had in store.

For time and time it almost seemed
that Brittney always asked,
"Can we please have a little dog,
a friend for me at last?"

We rescued you and gave you warmth,
a home, a yard, a bed.
For strong you grew and healthy
too, only fun-filled days ahead.

Our first dog. Our first man's best friend. What would our lives together be?
Only time would tell what the future held, we'd just have to wait and see.

From that day on and forever more
you would never leave our side,
You'd run and play and swim and
fetch and even go for a ride.

Your bed you made very comfortably and
with Brittney is where you slept,
She'd whisper in secret her fondest
dreams, every secret you tenderly kept.

Our family grew with the addition of Alex and Andi and you grew just the same, There was no limit to your kind love, they just added to your licking game.

As years went by, our friendship grew, that no one can deny, Through thick and thin you were always there, the time just seemed to fly.

A grey hair here and a grey hair there
your wisdom began to show,
And almost if by overnight
you quickly began to slow.

Old age they say is part of life
and for you it was just the same,
Then you couldn't run, you
couldn't play, the time was
near for the end of our game.

Our dog, our friend, our family, no
words express our thoughts,
We thank you for all your loyalty
and for all the fun you brought.

And now its clear, the answer's come to my question from when I was only seven, You'll be running and playing and fetching again because, "Yes", all dogs go to heaven.

"Where's Chulees Daddy?"

This was the difficult question that Andi asked when we returned from the veterinarian's office that night. "She's gone baby and she's not coming back" is all I could muster up. "She's sick?" she responded. I answered softly, "yes, but she's all better now, she went to doggy heaven."

As hard as this ordeal has been, we were fortunate to have had previous notice of our dog's illness. We had time to prepare and plan our young three-year old daughter for the inevitable. We had time to explain that she wouldn't be coming home. We even had just enough time to write this book together and share it with our Chulees before she departed.

But there were still questions.

In the heat of the moment, as I wrote, I didn't have time to extensively think of the implications of my story. I had reflected on a movie I had seen many years ago as a child, and the title and fundamental question came to mind. I didn't realize the difficulty of the next question to come.

"Where is heaven Daddy?"

Tough question. I answered as thoughtfully as I could.

"Heaven is a place where there is no more sickness, nor more pain. Heaven is a state of happiness. It is a state of eternal peace. Heaven for some is real and for others does not exist. Heaven is the fond memory we hold of a loved one we can no longer physically talk to or see. So when you remember Chulees and those memories bring you happiness, love, joy and even sadness, that is where heaven is." I asked, "where do you think heaven is." She answered, "it's where Chulees goes to play."

For a three year-old that question still remains.

Have you ever had to explain to a young child the concept of death? Have you ever been faced with the difficult talk of explaining *heaven*? How did you handle it? Let us know at **AlexAndiAdventures.com**

A Note from Alex and Andi

We hope you enjoyed the story of our
beloved four-legged friend.
Be happy because a new adventure
starts as another one ends.

Will the next be about grandma, grandpa, mom or dad?
Pick up your copy now and you're sure to be glad.

Don't wait because we have many stories to tell.
You can always check our website for updates as well.

We'll share additional stories, videos and even some pics,
Learn new things together and pick
up some really cool tricks.

We'd also love to hear the exciting news all about you,
So visit **AlexAndiAdventures.com** to
see what we have in store for you.

Also, please let us know that you enjoy our stories and care,
by leaving us comments, likes or even a share.

For our friendship together will grow
fond and only get better.
Who knows, Alex and Andi might even
send you a personal letter!

About The Author

Andrew L. Ramirez is the father of three beautiful girls (Brittney-19, Andrea-3 and Alexandra-1). He hopes to connect with families around the globe on a very personal level as he shares his true stories about his real family.

His stories for the Alex and Andi series are inspired by his two youngest. You can find out how to get free copies of his books by visiting **Facebook.com/AlexAndiAdventures**

You can also find his additional work on effectively parenting teens inspired by his teenage daughter Brittney by visiting **Facebook.com/TerrificTeenInstitute**

Made in the USA
Coppell, TX
21 September 2022

83488738R00021